The FIREPLACE
DESIGN Sourcebook

Melissa Cardona

Schiffer Publishing Ltd®

4880 Lower Valley Road, Atglen, PA 19310 USA

Library of Congress Cataloging-in-Publication Data

Cardona, Melissa.
    The fireplace design sourcebook / Melissa Cardona.
        p. cm.
    ISBN 0-7643-2283-4 (pbk.)
1. Fireplaces. 2. Interior decoration. I. Title.

NA3050.C37 2005
721'.8—dc22

2005011820

2

Designed by "Sue"
Type set in Atlantic Inline/Humanist521 BT

ISBN: 0-7643-2283-4
Printed in China

Cover photo courtesy of Harrison Design Associates.
Title page photo courtesy of Kelley Interior Design.
Back cover photo courtesy of HPBA and Tulikivi.

Published by Schiffer Publishing Ltd.
4880 Lower Valley Road
Atglen, PA 19310
Phone: (610) 593-1777; Fax: (610) 593-2002
E-mail: Info@schifferbooks.com

For the largest selection of fine reference books on this and related subjects, please visit our web site at
www.schifferbooks.com
We are always looking for people to write books on new and related subjects. If you have an idea for a book please contact us at the above address.

This book may be purchased from the publisher.
Include $3.95 for shipping.
Please try your bookstore first.

You may write for a free catalog.

In Europe, Schiffer books are distributed by
Bushwood Books
6 Marksbury Ave.
Kew Gardens
Surrey TW9 4JF England
Phone: 44 (0) 20 8392-8585; Fax: 44 (0) 20 8392-9876
E-mail: info@bushwoodbooks.co.uk
Free postage in the U.K., Europe; air mail at cost.

CONTENTS

INTRODUCTION

The art of fire has come a long way since the bygone days when it was a necessary part of everyday life. We no longer keep a fire burning morning till night to warm the home, prepare food, or heat water for bathing and washing clothes. Likewise, fireplaces are no longer requisite components in our modern homes, where appliances and central heat have taken over the duties once executed with a well-stoked fire. Today, a fireplace in the home is a luxury, an "extra" that can raise the resale value of a home. Nonetheless, most homeowners today opt for including that "extra," without which a home just doesn't seem complete.

The allure and appeal of a fireplace stems not from the marketability of a home. It's something more innate – the attraction and affinity for the warmth and light of dancing flames is at once primal and nostalgic. Most of us have no primordial memory of depending on fire for survival, but we can probably recall sitting in the glow of a fireplace with our family during the holidays or after a day spent playing in the snow.

In addition to that warm and fuzzy feeling they give us, fireplaces offer many advantages to homeowners. They can provide zone heating in frequently used rooms, cutting energy costs associated with heating an entire home. A fireplace enhances the atmospheric quality of a room and provides a focal point in a room's design. And with the abundance of hearth products on the market today, it's easy for homeowners to find a fireplace suited to their heating and decorating needs.

The hearth product industry has boomed in the last decade. Not only have hearth products become safer and more efficient, but consumers now have many more styles, colors, and decorative features from which to choose. It's important to decide what kind of product is right for you and for your home. The main types of products on the market today include gas and woodburning stoves and fireplaces, pellet stoves, and electric ambient heaters. Each type of hearth product presents unique advantages and disadvantages that should be considered carefully before making a purchasing decision. Such details should be explored with a knowledgeable hearth product dealer.

This book is intended as a design reference to help you find a style that appeals to you, and to give you inspiration for your own home's fireplace. A resource guide at the end of the book includes contact information for all the manufacturers, interior designers, and architects who contributed photographs for this book. Please visit their websites or call them for an even greater breadth of designs. For more information regarding hearth products, the Hearth, Patio, and Barbecue Association's website <www.hpba.org> provides a wealth of information.

MANTELS, HEARTHS, AND SURROUNDS
AN EXPLORATION OF MATERIALS AND DESIGNS

STONE

6

A stacked stone fireplace adds a historic dimension to a room decorated with contemporary art. A leather armchair with ottoman is a fireplace's perfect companion. *Courtesy of Sroka Design*

A stone chimney climbs the wall of a wood-paneled dining room fit for King Arthur and his knights. The stacked stone adds history and rustic appeal to the polished and crafted look of wood paneling. An arch was created in the surround by placing stones upright above the fireplace opening, which was set at a height to be visible from the dining room table. *Courtesy of Miller Stein Interior Design*

An Asian motif embellishes this beautiful gray and green soapstone fireplace. The hearth was constructed with a compartment to house wood and an ash drawer from which ashes can easily be collected and disposed. *Courtesy of HPBA and Tulikivi*

Opposite page:
Two reclaimed chestnut mantelshelves sit atop a cut stone fireplace with keystone arch. Hooks to hang fireplace tools were installed into the bottom mantelshelf. The paintings hung above the fireplace have textured surfaces, keeping with the room's modern yet rustic aesthetic. *Courtesy of Harrison Design Associates*

Large timbers were used in the mantel of a pewter-faced fireplace to complement the home's timber frame construction. Perfectly rectangular slabs of slate tile the surround, providing complement and contrast to the room's expansive wall of stone. *Courtesy of Harman Stove Co.*

Photography by Mark Finkenstaedt, www.mfpix.com

A gorgeous granite rubble fireplace surround is topped with a polished slab of monolithic black granite weighing 600 pounds. A thermal finished black granite hearth completes the design. *Courtesy of Hadrian Stone Masonry, Inc.*

A 4" Blue River tumbled blend veneer fireplace surround and hearth were applied over concrete block. The full masonry construction is accompanied by an oak mantel. The combination attractively dresses up a gas insert for a casual, yet stylish look. *Courtesy of Semco Distributing, Inc.*

Opposite page:
Rattan furnishings beautifully complement the look of a cut stone fireplace. An antique woven basket hung on the fireplace provides a focal point. *Courtesy of Harrison Design Associates*

Thin veneer offers the beauty of rustic-looking stone, especially with the addition of a chunky oak mantel. *Courtesy of Semco Distributing, Inc.*

Courtesy of Monessen Hearth Systems

A fieldstone veneer was chosen to complement the natural stone floor of this dining room. A single dark timber was used as the mantel to match the table.
Courtesy of HPBA and RSF Energy

Courtesy of HPBA and Selkirk, Inc.

Miniature recessed lights shine in luminous columns upon a colorful piece of abstract art. Sconces were hung on both sides of the stone surround to better display the stonemason's master craft. The gorgeous stone surround adds an earthy dimension to a room rich in polish and texture.
Courtesy of Miller Stein Interior Design

Stone native to this home's area was cut and stacked in a rectangular fireplace surround. The combination of textures and earthy colors creates an inviting and relaxing atmosphere is this master bedroom. *Courtesy of Harrison Design Associates*

Spotlights attached to a beam illuminate the upper area of soaring stone mantel, drawing attention to a hunter's prized catch. *Courtesy of Harman Stove Co.*

15

A reclaimed timber mantelshelf is the perfect companion for a gorgeous stone chimney. *Courtesy of Heatilator*

This arched woodburning fireplace is extremely efficient and stylish, set in a wall of stone with a log-constructed mantel. *Courtesy of Heat & Glo*

Built-in shelves flank a stone fireplace surround and circular hearth in a family room dominated by warm earth tones. *Courtesy of Heat & Glo*

Right:
A wall of flagstone stretches onto the floor as the hearth. A throw rug in golden tones complements the fireplace surround and adds a rustic touch to the room. *Courtesy of Travis Industries*

Large timbers form the mantel of a gas
fireplace set in stone for a rustic look.
Courtesy of Lennox Hearth Products

Stone rises from floor to ceiling for
dramatic and eye-catching effect.
Courtesy of Monessen Hearth Systems

The shape of the mantel is repeated in a moulded architectural element near the ceiling. The stone surround and exposed wooden ceiling add texture to neo-classical elements. *Courtesy of Travis Industries*

19

An oversized fireplace includes a cut bluestone surround that climbs from floor to ceiling. The stately design has a grand effect in a room that recalls days of yore. *Courtesy of Harrison Design Associates*

A great room requires a fireplace of just-as-great proportions to fill the space. Here, local fieldstone soars from floor to ceiling for a traditional look embellished by a timber mantel with a favorite quote carved in its façade. *Courtesy of Harrison Design Associates*

Opposite page:
Newer homes feature open floor plans, which offer ideal settings for see-thru fireplaces. Shelves to the side of a soaring stone fireplace sur-round take the place of a mantelshelf.
Courtesy of Heat & Glo

A wall of fieldstone gives the impression of a masonry fireplace, but houses a vent-free firebox instead. A ruddy-colored mantel brings out the warm tones of the stone. *Courtesy of Monessen Hearth Systems*

A piece of reclaimed timber was bolted into the wall to form the mantelpiece, while stone was used in the surround and hearth. Embossed wallpaper balances formality with the rustic look of the fireplace. *Courtesy of Travis Industries*

Opposite page, top:
Dark stone arches over the fireplace opening, stretching up over the entire wall and down to form a raised hearth. The thick texture and dark gray color of the stone have a gothic feel and contrast beautifully with pine framing found throughout the room. *Courtesy of Travis Industries*

Opposite page, bottom:
Fireplaces are popping up all over the home. See-thru fireplaces like this one are an especially good choice for an area between two rooms. *Courtesy of Heat & Glo*

A home rich in rustic details features a stone wall as the backdrop for a sand-colored enamel stove. *Courtesy of Harman Stove Co.*

25

A 1" stone veneer surrounds a wood/gas insert. The thin veneer can be applied virtually anywhere with correct preparation and without the structural support needed by a thicker veneer. *Courtesy of Semco Distributing, Inc.*

26

Reclaimed timber frames call for the use of a less polished material, like fieldstone, in the fireplace's design. Here, a native variety climbs from the hearth to the ceiling in a breathtaking display, while maintaining a feeling of coziness. *Courtesy of Harrison Design Associates*

During the warm months, a cast stone fireplace is filled with a cascade of dried flowers. *Courtesy of Harrison Design Associates*

Minimalist styling dictates the use of an austere cast concrete fireplace surround. *Courtesy of Solus Decor*

An ornate fireplace façade eliminates the need for other adornments like a painting or wreath. Cast stone provides texture and tradition to a room rich in classic styling. *Courtesy of HPBA and Pacific Energy*

28

A wide, black-framed mirror complements an elegant cast concrete surround in gray to create a suitable centerpiece for a room with contemporary styling. *Courtesy of Solus Décor*

Cast concrete is a versatile material that can be customized with colors and unique designs to reflect your personal tastes. Here, a fireplace surround is constructed from four separate pieces of cast concrete. *Courtesy of Flying Turtle Cast Concrete*

A classically designed fireplace was embellished with carvings of animals indigenous to the home's area. *Courtesy of Harrison Design Associates*

Blue walls breathe serenity into an airy space that is casual yet elegant. A pastel bouquet framed in gold sits atop the cast stone fireplace and adds a hint of pink to the room's color palette. *Courtesy of Harrison Design Associates*

31

32

Scagliola stone was used to construct a Provence-inspired fireplace, which, in combination with tropical furnishings and a minimalist aesthetic, produces a room rich in texture and interest.
Courtesy of Harrison Design Associates

A gray rug with gold accents unifies a cast stone fireplace and gold-colored walls and textiles.
Courtesy of Harrison Design Associates

33

A cast stone fireplace warms up this study on cold nights spent reading or catching up on work. *Courtesy of Harrison Design Associates*

Photography by Omar Salinas

A miniature version of Picasso's *Guernica* and flanking wall sconces adorn the wall above this cast concrete fireplace mantel. *Courtesy of Sroka Design*

An ornate cast stone mantel extends to the ceiling and adds a sense of history to this parlor. *Courtesy of Heatilator*

Concrete was cast with special coloring to give it a textured, aged appearance. Decorative concrete offers a vast array of decorative features that can be tailored specifically to your tastes. *Courtesy of Sroka Design*

37

BRICK

White moulding and brick add a traditional touch to a room with contemporary appeal. *Courtesy of Chris Barrett Design, Inc. and KAA Design Group*

An oversized wreath adorns a soaring brick mantel and chimney, which form the centerpiece of this gorgeous room. *Courtesy of the Brick Association of the Carolinas*

Photography by Dennis Nodine Photography

A metal gas insert set in a brick surround provides warmth and adds style to this room. *Courtesy of Jøtul North America*

Opposite page:
A wooden fireplace mantel was mounted on an unbroken wall of gray brick. The hearth was constructed using the same gray brick to create a sense of continuity.
Courtesy of Heatilator

A freestanding wood stove was inserted into an original masonry fireplace surrounded by brick. Slate tiles were spread out from the wall to form an unobtrusive hearth. *Courtesy of Jøtul North America*

40

Bricks create the backdrop for a white woodburning stove. *Courtesy of Jøtul North America*

An ornamental antique mirror crowns a walnut wood mantel handcrafted in a French vein. The mirror was chosen for its style, as well as for its size, in order to match the proportion of the room's large windows. *Courtesy of Harrison Design Associates*

Photography by Gordon Beall

A brick fireplace surround complements the home's historic architecture. Without much space under the eaves, a small mirror was chosen to adorn the wall above the mantel. *Courtesy of Sroka Design*

A fireplace made from brick with a stucco wash rises toward the ceiling in a hood-like construction. A broken pattern of bricks imitates the effect of an old fireplace worn with time. *Courtesy of Harrison Design Associates*

43

Faux columns extend from floor to ceiling and are echoed in the fireplace mantel for a neoclassical effect. A brick surround complements the look. *Courtesy of Lennox Hearth Products*

A very formal dining room features a wide fireplace. Originally constructed from brick, it was covered with moulded wood paneling to match the rest of the room, rising above the opening into a graceful gothic arch. Branches with leaves adorning the over mantel and fireplace surround are reminiscent of Asian flower art, in keeping with the Asian-inspired accessories that fill the room. *Courtesy of Pauline Vastardis Interiors*

Photography by Barry Halkin

This is the perfect setting for an avid hunter and outdoorsman to display a decorative collection of outdoor supplies. Fieldstone columns make a good companion to the brick surround and reclaimed timber mantel. *Courtesy of the Brick Association of the Carolinas*

Photography by Dennis Nodine Photography

The stove's vertical aspect, curved facade, and brushed stainless steel side panels give it a contemporary look. Convection heating, a small footprint, and excellent clearances to combustibles make this an ideal stove for small spaces. The stove features a bottom drawer for storage of gloves and other accessories. *Courtesy of Morsø and Hearthlink International, Randolph VT*

45

46

Opposite page:
The pecky cypress wood mantel and black slate surround create an austere look appropriate for this study. A nautical-inspired painting above the mantel maintains the room's subdued color palette. *Courtesy of Harrison Design Associates*

An oversized wood mantel was installed to complement the proportions of the room, dictated by large windows and a high ceiling. *Courtesy of Monessen Hearth Systems*

Victorian lamps and a gold-framed landscape painting complement the filigreed grate on the fireplace doors. Moulded wood trim painted white was used for the fireplace surround for a simple and elegant look. *Courtesy of Travis Industries*

47

Moulded panels cover the walls of a sitting room to create a formal look, as does the elegant white mantel. A ruddy fireplace surround complements the room's deep red walls and red and brown fabrics. *Courtesy of Travis Industries*

Wood paneling surrounds an entertainment center, is repeated in the fireplace mantel, and continues around the room. Flames impart ambient lighting in this entertainment room. *Courtesy of Travis Industries*

Light blue walls lend a sense of tranquility to this room. White sheers and accessories intensify the feeling of airiness, while the flickering flames of a gas stove have a centering effect. *Courtesy of Empire Comfort Systems, Inc.*

51

Black slate was chosen to complement a reclaimed cypress mantel. The beautiful grain of wood paneling provides ample interest in the room, which is brightened by a pair of floral-patterned armchairs. *Courtesy of Harrison Design Associates*

The entire room is paneled in reclaimed heart of pine, and features a black slate fireplace surround to provide contrast. *Courtesy of Harrison Design Associates*

52

54

Hand carved mahogany embraces a marble fireplace surround. *Courtesy of Harrison Design Associates*

Photography by Gordon Beall

A home's original carved marble fireplace with marble inlays was the basis for this room's wonderful gold and brown palette. *Courtesy Justine Sancho Interior Design*

56

A formal living room houses a fine collection of art and a fireplace that is itself a work of art. The antique Italian mantelpiece was purchased in Europe and features a mantelshelf carved from a single piece of solid stone weighing over 4,000 pounds. *Courtesy of Harrison Design Associates*

Photography by Tom Crane

This antique, early nineteenth century French mantel was the basis for the design of a formal living room. The rose-colored marble mantel with authentic ormolu gilding serves to center the grand, ethereal quality of the room, as well as establish its color palette. *Courtesy of Pauline Vastardis Interiors*

Opposite page:
This mahogany library features an antique Georgian style pewter mantel with travertine surround. A vivid painting was hung above the mantel, establishing the room's palette of primary colors, including an eclectic array of furnishings. *Courtesy of Harrison Design Associates*

Photography by Gordon Beall

An antique seventeenth century French limestone mantel anchors a room rich in textures and warm hues. *Courtesy Justine Sancho Interior Design*

Arches, columns, and gold gilding define a luxurious room rich in classical detailing, including an antique Italian marble fireplace. *Courtesy of Harrison Design Associates*

Photography by Stephen Meier Photography, www.stephenmeier.com

It was "love at first sight" when this room's designer spotted a wonderfully carved wood mantel in an antique shop. After hunting for something unusual to complement a beautiful bookcase in the living room, she knew that the mantel was "it" the moment she saw it. A mason was hired to reconfigure the firebox to accommodate the mantel's size and add a marble surround. The addition of green marble, a gold trimmed fireplace screen, and some magnolias completed the room's formal "Gone with the Wind" theme. *Courtesy of Sandra Murphy, IDS, Classic Design*

62

An exquisitely hand carved mahogany mantelpiece in the Georgian style includes a mirror with acanthus leaf trim and sanctuary marble surround. The historic design was modeled after a fire-place found in the Humphrey Sommers house in Charleston, South Carolina. *Courtesy of Harrison Design Associates*

An enormous living room stone fireplace features an intricate, three-dimensional screen cast in bronze. The designers envisioned a campfire in an aspen grove, and contracted an artist to cast bronze aspen branches that would hang over the fire. Glittering, polished leaves hang on the branch, and flutter in the rising heat of the gas fireplace's flames. The fireplace meets local code and permits the screen to have no glass. *Courtesy of Miller Stein Interior Design*

History is brought to life in a keeping room rich in textures. Reflecting the style of a French manor, the room features a Provence-inspired fireplace made from Scagliola stone. *Courtesy of Harrison Design Associates*

A gorgeous Arts and Crafts look is achieved with various wood stains and an eye-popping, multicolored stone tile fireplace surround. The burgundy-stained timber mantel contrasts magnificently. *Courtesy of Travis Industries*

This mantel was painted black to complement the craftsman style of the fireplace. Copper accent tiles add interest to the black surround. *Courtesy of Travis Industries*

Stylish fireplace doors keep the fire burning efficiently while adding décor to the room. *Courtesy of Heat & Glo*

With space allocated specifically for the television and stereo, this mantelpiece doubles as an entertainment center. *Courtesy of Lennox Hearth Products*

Dark wooden shelves and glass blocks create a unique look for this fireplace mantel and surround. *Courtesy of Heatilator*

Opposite page:
A mantel tiled in green with copper accents complements the arts and crafts styling of this masculine study. *Courtesy of Miller Stein Interior Design*

Moulded wood trim embellishes an arched, wall-mounted gas fireplace in keeping with the room's luxuriant French décor. *Courtesy of Heat & Glo*

Fine craftsmanship and carved detailing is reminiscent of the Old World. The stretch of ceiling above the fireplace is a darker shade to complement the mantelpiece. *Courtesy of Heat & Glo*

A spotlight shines on this fireplace to bring out the luminescence of mosaic tiles for a dramatic, eye-catching effect. *Courtesy of Crossville, Inc.*

A tiled border on the fireplace surround recalls design found in Tuscany. *Courtesy of HPBA and Pacific Energy*

The graceful curve of an arch adds elegance to this mantelpiece. *Courtesy of Lennox Hearth Products*

Glass glows in the presence of backlighting, adding further drama to a room steeped in imagination. The primal attraction to fire is strong in the heart of a cave, where medieval times come to life with authentic-looking accents. The mantel support columns were made from copper, fashioned with a claw on each side. *Courtesy of Design Specifications, Inc.*

A gas fireplace insert was incorporated into the wall and dressed up with a moulded cherry mantel for a masculine look. The stove's cast iron front and aluminum surround add classical appeal, while natural gas or propane capabilities provide flexible and convenient options. *Courtesy of Morsø and Hearthlink International, Randolph VT*

A wall of cast stone dominates the sitting room of a lakeside house, where a semi-circular hearth plays host to a small woodburning stove. *Courtesy of Travis Industries*

70

Cast concrete slabs tile the entire column of wall occupied by a fireplace and chimney. Simple and sleek, the fireplace needs little ornamentation to create a dramatic effect. *Courtesy of Solus Décor*

A corner fireplace was installed so the dancing light of flames would be visible from a patio. Stacked fieldstone was topped with flagstone tiles to create a sprawling hearth and add texture to this family room. *Courtesy of SFJ Architects*

A fireplace was imaginatively dressed in three columns of soapstone stacked with shelves. The circular metal vent pipe was painted to resemble gray stone, and a column of stone in the kitchen entryway brings cohesion to the open floor plan. *Courtesy of HPBA and Tulikivi*

Opposite page:
Dual sides of glass panes add versatility to a gas fireplace, which connects the living and dining rooms. Tiles above and below the fireplace replace the traditional mantel and hearth. *Courtesy of Heatilator*

A columned cut-out adds elegance and interest to the wall of a dual-sided gas fireplace. *Courtesy of Heatilator*

73

Rather than ending in a flat shelf, this custom mantel rises to a point for a very distinct look. A shelf was inset into the mantel to break up the visual expanse of wood. *Courtesy of Lennox Hearth Products*

Enormous tropical plants flank a towering chimney on protruding platforms that take the place of a mantel. Size matters in a room of such great proportions, and decorative features should be chosen carefully to complement the room's dimensions. *Courtesy of Rink Reynolds Diamond Fisher Wilson P.A.*

A custom corner construction houses this fireplace. In a large room with cathedral ceilings, the corner built-in features an inset arch with a tiled façade and a large painting. A single recessed light illuminates the area, creating a dramatic effect.when the rest of the room's lights are dimmed. *Courtesy of HPBA and Country Stoves*

A soaring sitting room provides a stunning setting for a hi-tech woodburning stove, which sits atop a simple hearth the color of sand. Darker tiles behind the stove create a non-combustible and geometrically appealing backdrop. *Courtesy of Rais & Wittus, Inc.*

The gears of time spin in a deco-inspired room. A mural stretches from floor to ceiling to provide a magnificent backdrop for a see-thru fireplace. *Courtesy Justine Sancho Interior Design*

Photography by Gordon Beall

This fireplace mantel was painted two-tone to accentuate hand-carved detailing. The room's neo-classical approach to design is accented with modern touches like two sleek armchairs and a geometric-inspired rug. *Courtesy of Sroka Design*

DECORATING IDEAS

78

Luxurious textures dictate the design of this room. A carved stone mantel features elegantly carved columns. *Courtesy of Rink Design Partnership, Inc.*

Opposite page:
An asymmetrically aligned collection of vases, a large Asian painting, and a hearty fireplace mantel fill the soaring wall of a vast living room.
Courtesy of Miller / Dolezal Design Group

79

This Italian Villa's grand living room is a study in symmetry, style, and scale. The Saturnia stone fireplace's opening was sized to incorporate a French, antique iron screen and keeps with the proportions of the room and furnishings. French Gothic armchairs flank the expansive fireplace, which is balanced on the opposite wall by a gilded Rococo mirror and hand-painted console. Furnishings were centered in the room to provide an anchor in the heart of the space, while allowing for circulation all around. *Courtesy of Vibha Hutchins, ASID*

Serving as a focal point in a great room with cathedral ceiling, a gas fireplace's mantel is echoed in the moulded architectural treatment that stretches to the roofline. *Courtesy of DESA™ Heating Products*

Photography by David F. Noyes Studios

A room of such large proportions deserves a fireplace to match. The swirling colors of the stone surround complement the wood grain of the oversized mantel and chimney, illuminated by a spotlight. *Courtesy of Rink Design Partnership, Inc.*

In a master bedroom, three recessed lights are positioned to shine on a far wall's three points of interest: two arched shelves and a hand carved mahogany fireplace with marble surround. *Courtesy of Harrison Design Associates*

A spotlight renders the fireplace and surrounding mantel the focal point of the room, setting a relaxing mood in tandem with the warm glow of flames. *Courtesy of HPBA and Heat & Glo*

Only a fireplace disrupts the gorgeous views from a wall of windows. An antique Chinese armoire was the inspiration for the room's Asian décor, asymmetrically arranged according to the principles of wabi-sabi. Spotlights shine away from the fireplace, which is lit at night by a tall lamp. *Courtesy of Simonton Windows*

A wood mantel is left practically bare, but for a pair of wall sconces and a small clock. Highly decorative wallpaper eliminates the need for other adornments. *Courtesy of Harrison Design Associates*

83

This sandstone mantel was hammered and chiseled to give it a textured appearance. White coral sits atop the mantel and complements the room's earthy sensibility. *Courtesy of Harrison Design Associates*

An ornamental mirror was too large to hang on the wall above the fireplace mantel, and was instead installed at an angle and attached to the wall with a chain for a Baroque effect and an interesting perspective of the room. *Courtesy of Harrison Design Associates*

Plants were pressed, framed in gold, and hung above the mantel in four rows of four. Flanked by a pair of wall sconces, the original work of art complements plant-inspired light fixtures in the room. *Courtesy of Harrison Design Associates*

Decorative wrought iron frames a wall-mounted fireplace with vines and leaves, echoing the arched shapes of the home's doorways. *Courtesy of HPBA and RSF Energy*

A collection of wilderness photography frames a distinctive fireplace. Set in walls of deep purple, the white mantel and black-and-white photographs are striking. *Courtesy of Lennox Hearth Products*

85

Paintings hung at uneven levels above the fireplace mantel engage the angled ceiling in a dialog. Black floor tiles scattered among dominant beige ones add to the effect. *Courtesy of Lennox Hearth Products*

Black-and-white photographs framed in black set the backdrop for a freestanding gas stove. *Courtesy of Jøtul North America*

A towering fireplace provides the focus of the room's furnishings. A pair of iron coal scuttles fashioned to look like Chinese guard dogs flank the cast stone fireplace. Torches bearing lemon leaves and perching angels highlight the mantel, while a mid-sixteenth century tapestry fragment acts as a focal point. The room achieves an earthy character and rich ambiance with an antique Lavar Kerman rug, refractory table, and custom iron chandeliers with Venetian candlestick torchieres. *Courtesy of Vibha Hutchins, ASID*

Opposite page:
An austere wood mantel and honed marble surround are dramatically dressed up with a mirror framed by tree roots. *Courtesy of Harrison Design Associates*

A formal living room just isn't complete without a fireplace. Here, a slightly elevated black hearth climbs the wall to surround the fireplace opening. An understated white mantel with elegant moulding is crowned by a gold-framed mirror, which offers a unique perspective of the room and complements other gold accents found around the room. *Courtesy of Kelley Interior Design*

An alcove above the mantel provides the perfect place to show off a treasured piece of art. *Courtesy of Heatilator*

89

Decorative tiles and a hood embellish this woodburning fireplace, set in between two white columns that complement the room's crown moulding. *Courtesy of Harman Stove Co.*

Photography by Barry Halkin

Opposite page, top:
The contrast of an off white crème marfil surround and gold-framed mirror against the dark walnut built-in draws attention to the fireplace. Walnut burled elements embellish the mantel, which rises toward the wall in a hood-like element. *Courtesy of Pauline Vastardis Interiors*

Opposite page, bottom:
Custom carving embellishes a cut stone travertine mantel in this formal living room. Original artwork in a gold frame adds color to the fireplace, unifying it with furnishings and accessories around the room. *Courtesy of Harrison Design Associates* The contrast of an off white crème marfil surround and gold-framed mirror against the dark walnut built-in draws attention to the fireplace. Walnut burled elements embellish the mantel, which rises toward the wall in a hood-like element. *Courtesy of Pauline Vastardis Interiors*

Wall sconces flank a large painting of docked sailboats. The cast stone of the fireplace mantel and hearth stretches to the ceiling to create a focal point in the room. *Courtesy of Rink Design Partnership, Inc.*

Lively furnishings and a colorful rug offset an understated mantel. Notice how the fireplace insert, which was smaller than the original fireplace's opening, was installed slightly to one side to allow space for hanging fireplace tools. *Courtesy of Miller Stein Interior Design*

93

A beautiful green onyx surround and hearth break the continuity of and provide interest to handcrafted walnut paneling. *Courtesy of Harrison Design Associates*

95

Expansive windows are balanced by a towering fireplace mantel that tapers toward the ceiling. The fireplace's buff bricks in a herringbone pattern are echoed in the woven design of a tabletop lamp. *Courtesy of Rink Design Partnership, Inc.*

Sienna Italian marble surrounds a fireplace in a room with walls papered in articles from Italian newspapers. *Courtesy of Harrison Design Associates*

A fireplace surround's gold mosaic tiles glitter like a necklace to match decorative accents above the mantel that twinkle in the light of the fire. An antique Venetian mirror crowns the complete ensemble with a sparkling effect. *Courtesy Justine Sancho Interior Design*

Opposite page, top:
Lighting is an important consideration when design-ing around a fireplace. Here, wall sconces and recessed lights highlight treasured paintings, and spotlights illuminate the deep recesses of a soaring ceiling. *Courtesy of Rink Design Partnership, Inc.*

Opposite page, bottom.
Windows, floor to ceiling, reveal the ocean views that inspired this room's décor. A sailboat floats atop a cast concrete mantel and is framed by a recessed wall tiled in cream and tan. *Courtesy of Simonton Windows*

Right:
A built-in unit houses a fireplace and entertainment system, providing plenty of shelf space to display an assortment of decorative items. *Courtesy of Simonton Windows*

Below:
Cozy chairs provide retreat, especially in the warm embrace of a working fireplace. Plants around the room complement fern-covered textiles and add color to a room dominated by neutral tones. *Cour-tesy of Ellen Dunn*

99

A black polished surround adds a sleek touch to the neoclassical hand-carved wood mantel. Black accessories around the room also provide a contemporary spin to neoclassical detailing. *Courtesy of Harrison Design Associates*

101

The fireplace surround was chosen to add contrast and complement the room's dark teal leather couch. The polished granite was also used for the hearth, and reflects the flicker of orange flames for an interesting effect. *Courtesy of Sroka Design*

A Scagliola stone fireplace with a gothic-inspired arch is the heart of an English Tudor style study.
Courtesy of Harrison Design Associates

The colors of the walls and furnishings bring out light blue and brown accents in the fireplace surround's stone tiles. *Courtesy of HPBA and Heatilator*

A brown enameled pellet stove adds polish to the clean lines of contemporary styling. *Courtesy of Harman Stove Co.*

A dark palette and luscious animal prints add exotic flair to this ambient room. *Courtesy of Harman Stove Co.*

Windows frame a gas fireplace with a black marble surround to create this room's stunning centerpiece. *Courtesy of Heatilator*

The rich combination of colors and textures lends an opulent air to this formal, yet cozy, living room. Notice the graceful decorative motif that adorns the pellet stove insert. *Courtesy of Harman Stove Co.*

This pellet stove automatically ignites when the room temperature falls below a set temperature. The stove's monitoring function keeps the room a constant, comfortable temperature. Gold trim and a tile top add form to function. *Courtesy of Harman Stove Co.*

A powerful gas stove is capable of comfortably heating a sitting room that opens to the foyer and second story hallway. *Courtesy of HPBA and Quadra-Fire*

Ruddy earth tones and lush foliage add tropical style to an opulent living room rich in texture. *Courtesy of Heatilator*

105

An antique French art deco firescreen provides flair to an austere fireplace srround. *Courtesy of Chris Barrett Design, Inc.*

106

A wood mantel with black granite surround echoes the neoclassical columns used in the doorways throughout this home. *Courtesy of Harrison Design Associates*

Dinners by the fire are luxuriant in the company of opulent antique furnishings and accessories. A brown marble surround is the perfect complement to an ornately carved crème marfil mantel. *Courtesy Justine Sancho Interior Design*

A cast plaster, faux-painted mantel looks hand-carved, and was combined with a marble surround to go hand-in-hand with this formal living room's classic styling. The rich, earthy tones of the fireplace ground the room's predominant gold tones. *Courtesy of Sroka Design*

Photography by F & E Schmidt

108

Lavish and regal, a formal living room seems to belong in a French palace. A custom-made mantel adorned with gold detailing was hand-painted with a patina that gives the impression of history. *Courtesy Justine Sancho Interior Design*

Two bouquets of flowers and a family portrait adorn a neoclassical wood mantel with marble surround. *Courtesy of Harrison Design Associates*

Opposite page:
Carved Italian marble makes a stunning appearance in
this grand salon as a custom-designed fireplace and
overmantel. The fireplace is open to the adjacent
hallway. *Courtesy of Harrison Design Associates*

111

A room filled with antiques features a hand carved mahogany mantel with
black-and-white marble surround. *Courtesy of Harrison Design Associates*

Historic tiles feature sailing
ships and frame the original
stone of a historic home's
fireplace. A painting above
the mantel continues the
nautical theme and glows
golden in its own spotlight.
Courtesy of Sroka Design

112

A carved mantel in white
carrera marble is classically
appealing, offering a simple
centerpiece in the midst of
ornate décor. *Courtesy of
Sroka Design*

Sand-colored marble flooring is used in the fireplace surround, embraced in a classically elegant mantel. *Courtesy of Travis Industries*

Center left:
With a low profile hearth design and a herringbone brick pattern, a vent-free firebox gives the impression of a traditional masonry fireplace. *Courtesy of Monessen Hearth Systems*

113

Wrought iron detailing on the fireplace screen adds contrast to a room rich in neutral tones. *Courtesy of Mendota Hearth Products*

This ornate, carved mantelpiece fits the luxurious, classic look of the room. *Courtesy of Lennox Hearth Products*

Native stone was used in the construction of this kitchen's handcrafted fireplace with a solid timber mantel bracketed by real deer antlers. Red and gold pears framed in gold add a punch of color to the fireplace. *Courtesy of Harrison Design Associates*

This small but powerful stove is the ideal choice for a small room, and is available in a wood or coal-burning model. Here, a wall of stone provides a non-combustible backdrop for the heat-radiating stove. *Courtesy of Morsø and Hearthlink International, Randolph VT*

A small, rustic cabin in the woods features a small gas stove in the corner to save space and warm things up. A simple hearth was constructed by placing six stone tiles on the floor beneath the stove. *Courtesy of Travis Industries*

A beautiful stone veneer was used as the backdrop for a fireplace and its mantel, which was made from a log saved during the construction of the home. *Courtesy of HPBA and Lexington*

A woodburning stove sits in the corner of this log cabin, dressed in a background of large, smooth stones. A hearth was constructed of smaller, flatter stones, which were also used in the mantelshelf. *Courtesy of Travis Industries*

Cultured stone forms the hearth and climbs the wall for a rustic look. A golden-colored timber was mounted to the wall as a mantelshelf. *Courtesy of Travis Industries*

Squares of poplar bark tile the area above a timber mantel, accenting the rustic stone fireplace. *Courtesy of Harrison Design Associates*

Ornate furnishings and accessories combined with a fieldstone fireplace and timber mantel create a space that is opulent, yet cozy. Sconces above the mantel match those found throughout the rest of the house, as well as a light fixture made from antlers. *Courtesy of Harrison Design Associates*

Opposite page:
Timber framing and a fireplace covered in smooth river stone add rustic flair to a grand space. *Courtesy of Harrison Design Associates*

A vent-free gas stove with vintage styling complements the collected country look of this room, but offers modern convenience with virtually maintenance-free operation. *Courtesy of Empire Comfort Systems, Inc.*

This corn stove can be altered to burn pellets – the perfect choice for a farmhouse dressed in cozy country attire. *Courtesy of Harman Stove Co.*

The original fireplace in a house built during colonial times produced smoky fires, so these homeowners installed a free-standing wood stove there – maintaining the look and warmth they desired. *Courtesy of Jøtul North America*

The original fireplace in an old farmhouse was given new life when a woodburning stove was installed there. Sunshine was added to the room with the yellow trim and mantelshelf. *Courtesy of Travis Industries*

Photography by Gordon Beall
The rustic look of a stone fireplace and wide planked wood flooring is complemented by the formality of the room's furnishings, a baby grand piano, and hand-painted murals. The effect is perfect for a country manor estate. *Courtesy of Sroka Design*

122

Photography by Gordon Beall

A wood mantelpiece was mounted to the wall of a stone fireplace and decorated with tole urns. The image hanging above the mantelshelf indicates this homeowner's love of horses. *Courtesy of Sroka Design*

Opposite page:
Made with an authentic-looking stone veneer, the corner fireplace adds texture and rustic appeal to a room decorated in Southwestern accessories, without the cost of real stone. *Courtesy of Eldorado Stone*

125

A reclaimed timber mantel sits atop the fireplace's stone surround to create a rustic look full of understated elegance. *Courtesy of Chris Barrett Design, Inc.*

Opposite page:
Warmth and flickering firelight add even more coziness to a room rich in earthy textures and tribal woven art. *Courtesy of Harman Stove Co.*

Terracotta tiles frame a direct-vent gas fireplace for an earthy look that works especially well in rooms decorated in southwestern style. *Courtesy of HPBA and Martin Hearth & Heating*

Curves are an attractive feature in the shapes of the fireplace and raised hearth. *Courtesy of Heatilator*

127

This gas fireplace has a unique southwest design that adds character to any room. In the kitchen, roosters adorn the shelves of an adobe-constructed mantel. *Courtesy of Heat & Glo*

Southwest styling is defined by a unique adobe mantel and chimney. *Courtesy of Heatilator*

A bright red armchair punctuates a room rich in subdued tones of gray. The fireplace was situated off center to add interest. *Courtesy of Solus Décor*

Opposite page:
Decorative stainless steel inlays enhance the modern design of an elegant stove. *Courtesy of Rais & Wittus, Inc.*

A tall black column adds function and form to a great room. The column houses the fireplace's venting system, while adding contrast to the room's light colors and horizontal crossbeams. *Courtesy of HPBA and Dimplex*

This stove's sleek lines complement the room's fusion of retro and contemporary styling. *Courtesy of Rais & Wittus, Inc.*

A mosaic glass fireplace surround shimmers on an earth-colored wall. Shelves were randomly hung above the fireplace to keep with the room's contemporary styling, and are lit up at night by a distinctive light fixture. *Courtesy of Harrison Design Associates*

A nickel-faced gas stove mounted into the wall provides an elegant complement to the study's clean lines. *Courtesy of Travis Industries*

132

Suspended above the ground, this ultra modern stove
can be rotated 360 degrees and enjoyed from any angle.
Courtesy of Rais & Wittus, Inc.

Opposite page, top:
Modernity meets tradition in a sleek fireplace surround
made from cast concrete slabs. *Courtesy of Solus Décor*

Opposite page, bottom:
Rather than the traditional look of logs, this gas stove
feautres a dramatic stone sculpture for a unique look.
Courtesy of Rais & Wittus, Inc.

133

A slab marble fireplace surround accented by a stainless steel fireplace insert was included in a mahogany paneled room for a fresh effect. The contemporary look of the fireplace creates a dynamic look within the traditional style of wood paneling. *Courtesy of Harrison Design Associates*

This wood stove lends retro styling to a vivid, contemporary room. *Courtesy of Harman Stove Co.*

A shiny black hearth accents the copper fireplace surround to achieve a zenful focal point in an Asian-inspired den. *Courtesy of Lennox Hearth Products*

A half wall was built to accommodate a peninsula fireplace. A simple black surround and unadorned setting are in keeping with the room's contemporary styling. *Courtesy of Lennox Hearth Products*

Straight lines and neutral colors produce a clean and attractive minimalist look. *Courtesy of HPBA and Doverra*

Stainless steel has a dramatic effect when used as a fireplace mantel, reflecting the dancing flames of a wood fire. A red painting and other decorative accents add further drama to the space. *Courtesy of Lennox Hearth Products*

The smooth curves of a wave-shaped fireplace add movement to a room. The custom design of a cast concrete fireplace surround can be tailored to meet any style. *Courtesy of Flying Turtle Cast Concrete*

Stainless steel frames glare-free glass in this attractive wood-burning stove. The non-catalytic stove includes a convenient wood storage chamber, and is an excellent addition to a room with contemporary style. *Courtesy of Pacific Energy*

BREAKING WITH TRADITION
HEARTH PRODUCTS THROUGHOUT THE HOME

A tower of flames spins dramatically upward in this truly unique work of fire art. Not only does this hearth product provide a mesmerizing show, but offers a comfortable level of heat for intimate spaces. *Courtesy of Heat & Glo*

A shelf was built to serve as this fireplace's mantel and provide function in the adjacent dining room. *Courtesy of Lennox Hearth Products*

The use of a bold color for this fireplace surround creates a focal point in the sitting room. On the opposite side a different color tile was used to complement the dining room's décor. *Courtesy of Lennox Hearth Products*

The chimney of a direct-vented gas fireplace rises through the top of a pony wall, which also houses a flat screen plasma television. *Courtesy of Lennox Hearth Products*

Opposite page:
Views on two sides of a vent-free gas fireplace allow people in the kitchen and family room to enjoy the glow and warmth of the fire. *Courtesy of DESA™ Heating Products*

Instead of a raised hearth, stone tiles the area of wall and floor below the fireplace in a cozy sitting room. *Courtesy of Heatilator*

Free of a venting system, this multi-view fireplace was installed into a tiered pony wall that serves to partially separate the two levels of the room. *Courtesy of Lennox Hearth Products*

141

Whether at the bar, lounging on the sofa, or shooting stick, everybody can enjoy the warm glow of this game room's corner fireplace. *Courtesy of Miller / Dolezal Design Group*

A corner woodburning fireplace adds a touch of coziness and primordial appeal to this high-tech home theater. A raised hearth and tile border were included in the fireplace design to make it a focal point. *Courtesy of Heatilator*

A corner cabinet contains a gas fireplace, saving space and adding ambiance in this dining room. *Courtesy of Travis Industries*

A window perfectly crowns the gas fireplace of an office full of clean lines and a crisp look. Although the study is a traditional spot for a fireplace, a modern office is better suited for a modern hearth product. *Courtesy of Heatilator*

BEDROOMS

Dark furnishings and accessories punctuate a room dominated by white and beige. A classically elegant mantel would complement any décor. *Courtesy of Heatilator*

A gas fireplace makes this bedroom a welcoming retreat, where the day's worries disappear with the flicker of flames. The peninsula design allows access from both the bed and sitting area of the master bedroom. *Courtesy of Heatilator*

A white mantel frames a thin marble surround and filigreed metal glass doors for a delicate look in the bedroom. *Courtesy of Heatilator*

Opposite page:
A custom-made cherry wood mantelpiece matches paneling used throughout this master bath. Pocket doors above the mantelshelf slide back to reveal a television. *Courtesy of Design Specifications, Inc.*

Inserting a gas fireplace into the area below a bay window saved valuable space in this small master bedroom. *Courtesy of Heatilator*

A see-thru fireplace provides warmth and glow to a master suite – including the master bath. *Courtesy of Lennox Hearth Products*

BATHROOMS

Crowned by a recessed wall with a
gas fireplace, a bubbling tub in the
glow of candle and firelight is the
ultimate therapy after a long day.
Courtesy of Heatilator

Left:
Stone is used inside this wall-
mounted gas fireplace, comple-
menting the bath's caramel-
colored wood and arts and crafts
styling. *Courtesy of Travis Industries*

Opposite page:
This luxuriant master bath offers a
sensual feast. Rich textures fill the
room from floor to ceiling, and a gas
fireplace provides warmth and
ambience. A distressed maple
mantel frames an ivory rustic
cobbled travertine surround. An
elegantly shaped niche above the
fireplace provides display space.
Courtesy of Design Specifications, Inc.

150

A black wall-mounted gas fireplace is an attractive addition to tan walls with white wainscoting. Including a cherry table and decorative items in the bath adds coziness and style. *Courtesy of Travis Industries*

The original linen closet in a master bath was replaced by a see-thru fireplace and adjacent shelves with the installation of a Jacuzzi bathtub. *Courtesy of HPBA and Heat & Glo*

151

Luxury is no stranger to this bath, where mauve and gray tiling embrace a Jacuzzi and wall-mounted gas fireplace. *Courtesy of Travis Industries*

This direct vent gas insert is installed directly into the wall and features a small mantel where decorative accessories like candles and glass bottles can be displayed. *Courtesy of HPBA and Country Stoves*

Two columns invite the master of the house into a throne of relaxation and comfort. A wall-mounted gas fireplace warms the air and provides a soft glow to further incite serenity. *Courtesy of Travis Industries*

A stone-encased wood oven completes the look of a
kitchen designed to transport its owners back to nature.
Distressed wood finishes on the cabinetry, painted wood
plank floors, and the fireplace all contribute to a cozy
atmosphere full of modern amenities. The wood oven
can be used to make pizza, or to warm up the room on
cold days. *Courtesy of Plain & Fancy Custom Cabinetry*

155

A simple mantelpiece plays host to
decorative and colorful accessories, acting as the room's focal
point. *Courtesy of Heatilator*

A direct vent gas fireplace was installed beneath a kitchen window and topped with a display shelf. *Courtesy of Heatilator*

Stone tiles demarcate a wood-burning fireplace's space in a half wall between the kitchen and breakfast nook. *Courtesy of Heatilator*

Scandinavian style is best accompanied by a simple black firebox set into the wall. An opening below the fireplace provides a place to store wood. *Courtesy of Rais & Wittus, Inc.*

A rectangular alcove was included in the design of this kitchen's fireplace to add interest and a decorative touch to the plain white wall. *Courtesy of Lennox Hearth Products*

Perfect for the kitchen, this unique gas fireplace features a flip-down warming shelf on the door. *Courtesy of Heat & Glo*

A sunroom was blessed with the addition of a stacked stone fireplace to complement the use of other natural textures throughout the room. An original bronze sculpture adorns the fireplace without overpowering the beauty of the stone, while also setting off the black metal screen used to cover the fireplace opening. *Courtesy of Sroka Design*

This indoor/outdoor gas fireplace can be enjoyed from the family room and the patio at the same time. Special engineering ensures that no heat will escape from the direct vent system. *Courtesy of Heat & Glo*

Set into a wall of white-painted bricks, this stove offers stylish simplicity and cozy warmth to a sunroom. *Courtesy of Rais & Wittus, Inc.*